Presented to

Ma

From

Chuck & Chris

Date

12/27/09

EXPERIENCE
THE PRESENCE OF
GOD

SPIRITUAL REFLECTIONS *with* IMAGES
from the HOLY LAND

KEN DUNCAN

INTEGRITY
PUBLISHERS®

Nashville
www.IntegrityPublishers.com

Because of Christ and our faith in him,

we can now come fearlessly into God's presence,

assured of his glad welcome.

EPHESIANS 3:12 NLT

Your Invitation

God has extended his personal invitation to you—

yes, you—to step fearlessly into His Presence.

What a privilege and honor—and all because of

His great love for you, expressed most fully in

the gift of His Son Jesus Christ.

My prayer is that you will experience God in a

new and profound way as you reflect on

what His Word says to you—and as you savor

the wonder and beauty of the very places,

the very land where Jesus walked.

Ken Duncan.

THE JUDEAN WILDERNESS, ISRAEL
Jesus was led into the Judean wilderness to be tempted.

So God led them along a route through the wilderness
toward the Red Sea,
and the Israelites left Egypt like a marching army.

EXODUS 13:18 NLT

Trust God's Leading

The day had finally arrived! After more than four hundred years, the sons and daughters of Abraham were to be set free from the brutal hand of Pharaoh. They would trade in the sun and sand of Egypt for the milk and honey of Canaan, their promised land. A short walk from Egypt around the coast of the Mediterranean Sea would bring them safely home. But Moses made a right turn out of Egypt and headed straight into the wilderness of Sinai. Little did the people know that God was leading them on a wilderness road to protect them from the ferocious Philistines who would have beaten them back to Egypt (Exodus 13:17).

It was in the wilderness that the family of Israel came to know their God for who He really was: Guide, Protector, Provider, and Lover of their souls.

If you are on a similar path through uncertain terrain, trust His leading—and look for Him. Like a luxurious tree offering shade in the wilderness, God was there for Israel—and He will be there for you.

Blessing in Abundance

'For I will pour out water on the thirsty land
And streams on the dry ground;
I will pour out My Spirit on your offspring
And My blessing on your descendants;
And they will spring up among the grass
Like poplars by streams of water.'

ISAIAH 44:3–4 NASB

—◦◦✦◦◦—

Life hangs precariously in the balance when water grows scarce. And for the first time in history, water is becoming a precious commodity all over the world—not just in arid regions.

The prophets of old foresaw a time when God's blessing would course through the world like rivers of crystal water—cooling, satisfying, and purifying. Water was a symbol of the Holy Spirit because of its seemingly never-ending abundance and its ability to produce life wherever it flowed. Such is the way of the Holy Spirit. He is infinite and life-giving; there is no heart too hard for Him to soften and cause life to spring up in abundance.

If you find your own soul dry and lifeless, ask the Holy Spirit to wash over you and fill you to overflowing with His presence. Given the Spirit's infinite abundance, your spiritual life need never hang in the balance.

BANIAS WATERFALL, CAESAREA PHILIPPI, ISRAEL
Jesus and His disciples would have seen this waterfall on their journey through the Caesarea Philippi area.

My sheep recognize my voice.
I know them, and they follow me.

JOHN 10:27 MSG

Hearing and Following

Sheep shuffle along—heads bobbing, bells tinkling—following the wall of wool directly in front of them. Although it looks like they're following the shepherd, most of the time they can't even see him. Instead, they're watching their step over tricky terrain, trusting that the shepherd is there, leading, whether seen or not.

They're really following his voice. His trademark yells, whistles, and commands—*the sound of his voice, and his alone*—is what keeps them relaxed and secure, knowing that green grass and still waters will soon be theirs.

There are thousands of shepherds' voices in today's world, but only One that is "the way, the truth, and the life" (John 14:6). The challenge is to listen to that voice enough so we can pick it out amidst all the others that say, "Follow me." The longer you follow Jesus, the more recognizable His voice will become to you. Even in times when you can't see Him clearly, as long as He is your Shepherd, you will always be able to hear His voice—and follow it.

When Life Is a Cliff-Hanger

When we read the four Gospels and see the things Jesus did, we are sometimes tempted to think of Him like a first-century Houdini—a magician who astounded people by his sleight of hand. When religious leaders in Nazareth were enraged over His teaching and tried to kill Him by throwing Him off a cliff, the Bible says He just "walked right through the crowd and went on His way."

How? Did He become invisible? Did He cause the others to go temporarily blind so they couldn't see Him? In our scientific age, we are often easily confused by events that lack rational explanations. We don't like being out of the loop. But if we insist on explaining everything God does, we demystify who He is. The point is not how Jesus escaped, but that He escaped—something only God could have done.

The next time your life turns into a cliff-hanger, don't try to figure out how Jesus can rescue you. Just be thankful that He can and will.

THE MOUNT OF THE PRECIPICE, NEAR NAZARETH, ISRAEL

Jesus enraged some of the inhabitants of Nazareth by His preaching. They tried to throw Him off this precipice to kill Him, but Jesus was supernaturally delivered from this fate.

They got up, drove him out of the town, and

took him to the brow of the hill on which the town was built,

in order to throw him down the cliff.

But he walked right through the crowd and went on his way.

LUKE 4:29–30 NIV

God of the Second Chance

Jesus repeated the question:
"Simon son of John, do you love me?"
"Yes, Lord," Peter said, "you know I love you."
"Then take care of my sheep," Jesus said.

JOHN 21:16 NLT

The story is told of an employee whose mistake cost his company a hundred thousand dollars. When he volunteered to resign, the owner said, "Are you kidding? It cost me a fortune for you to learn an important lesson. If you leave, I'll have to spend the same amount teaching the next person the same thing!"

The employer believed in second chances and knew that people are often wiser and better after failing than before. The same can be said of Jesus, the Lord of the Second Chance.

Peter had failed miserably as a disciple. Once he rebuked Jesus (Matthew 16:22) and then denied he even knew Him when the stakes got high (Matthew 26:69-75). Yet after the resurrection, by the Sea of Galilee, Jesus called Peter back into service. He didn't focus on the past by asking Peter if he was sorry he had sinned. Instead, He looked to the future by asking, "Peter, do you love me?" and then made Peter the chief shepherd among His followers.

All Jesus wants to know about what you did yesterday is whether or not you love Him today.

Thought to be where Jesus appeared to His disciples.

Saving the Best for First

So Abraham ran back to the tent and said to Sarah,
"Quick! Get three measures of your best flour,
and bake some bread."

GENESIS 18:6 NLT

—◦◦◦✦◦◦◦—

God has never been shy about dropping in unannounced, when we least expect Him.

The Lord, accompanied by two angels, stopped by Abraham's and Sarah's tent one day to deliver the news that they would be having a baby. But before Abraham received that promise—and seemingly before he knew it was the Lord who was visiting—he shifted into hospitality mode. He washed his visitors' dusty feet with water, had Sarah use their best flour to bake bread, roasted a tender young calf, and served it all to the three strangers with milk and curds. They gave their best for people they didn't know and served God in the process.

The Bible warns us about failing to "show hospitality to strangers, for some who have done this have entertained angels without realizing it" (Hebrews 13:2). Since God never drops by dressed as we might imagine Him to, we should give our best to everyone.

LADY COOKING BREAD, NAZARETH VILLAGE, NAZARETH, ISRAEL

We Should Be Overwhelmed

If God gives such attention to the

appearance of wildflowers —

most of which are never even seen —

don't you think he'll attend to you,

take pride in you, do his best for you?

MATTHEW 6:30 MSG

—◦✦◦—

Some days the sky at sunset looks like God's palette into which He dips His brush to paint the next day. The wild flowers look like a carpet flung down from the sky to cover the hillsides—heaven on earth for tiny pollen collectors. And in the sea swims a kaleidoscopic array of fins and gills in a world all their own.

We look at what God has done in nature and marvel at His creativity: "God is so great! Look what He has made!" Yet when we look in the mirror, we are less than impressed. Why are we over-whelmed with creation and under-whelmed with ourselves, the pinnacle of creation itself?

Daily God paints the sky, carpets the earth, and maintains the animals. Yet we have a hard time believing He will take care of us. Look around … be in awe … and believe.

SUNRISE THROUGH FLOWERS ON THE MOUNT OF BEATITUDES
This is the area where Jesus preached His famous Sermon on the Mount.

SUNRISE AT BETHLEHEM, PALESTINE
The hills in the background may be where the angel appeared to the shepherds to tell them of Jesus' birth.

"But you, Bethlehem Ephrathah, though you are small among the clans of Judah, out of you will come for me one who will be ruler over Israel, whose origins are from of old, from ancient times."

MICAH 5:2 NIV

No Small Places

God often begins big things in small, out-of-the-way places. Bethlehem was such a place—a mere blip on the radar of the Holy Land. Yes, it was the City of David, but that's only because David's family lived there when he was anointed to be the king of Israel.

Bethlehem always existed in the shadow of Jerusalem, five miles to its northeast. Bethlehem was a bedroom community, a suburb. Hardly the main attraction in the land of Judah. Until, that is, God sent an anonymous couple there to give birth to Jesus. That one commonplace event—the birth of a child—changed Bethlehem forever. Zechariah the prophet was right when he said how much joy small beginnings bring to God (Zechariah 4:10).

Many of us live in small, out-of-the-way places—or so it seems to us. But there are no small places with God. Only people and places where God wants to do really big things in His time and His way.

Signs of Faith

"Don't be alarmed," he said.
"You are looking for Jesus the Nazarene,
who was crucified. He has risen! He is not here.
See the place where they laid him."

MARK 16:6 NIV

Go to the Garden Tomb in Jerusalem today and you'll see a sign on the door: "He is not here—for He is risen." Of course, the tomb Jesus was buried in was covered by a huge stone, not a wooden door. And most assuredly, when the women arrived at the tomb to anoint Jesus' body, there was no sign telling them what had happened.

Yes, there was an angel who explained that Jesus had risen. But that probably only complicated matters. Mark says the women fled, "trembling and bewildered." Signs are brief, concise, and to the point. A sign would have been easier than an angel. But God doesn't always do what is easiest for us (Isaiah 55:8-9). He just does what He does and leaves us with our faith instead of a sign explaining what has happened.

But that's how we grow—by faith, not by sight (2 Corinthians 5:7). So instead of looking for a sign, *be* a sign to others that God can be trusted.

TOMB DOOR, THE GARDEN TOMB

So that from the rising of the sun to the place of its setting

men may know there is none besides me.

I am the LORD, and there is no other.

Think of God

We constantly need reminding. A generation ago people used the proverbial string tied around a finger to remind them of something important. Today we use sticky notes, day planners, digital voice recorders, emails, and telephone voice messages. The older we get, the more of those we might have to employ.

Not only do we forget our personal stuff, but our memory about God fails as well. To help us remember, He gives us reminders—beginning with the rainbow after the Flood. Whenever we see a rainbow, we're reminded that there will never again be waters to cover the earth in judgment (Genesis 9:13-16).

The rising of the sun and the setting of the sun are another reminder about the God of Abraham, Isaac, and Jacob—He alone is God. There are not two suns, one that rises and one that sets. Nor is there more than one God.

The next time you witness the glory of the sun rising or setting, be glad that you know the only true God.

Traversing Dark Valleys

When it was the City of David, ravines and valleys surrounded Jebus (Jerusalem) on three sides—defendable high ground. On the east side, an intermittent brook, the Kidron, trickled along the bottom of a sharp-sided ravine. In Jesus' day, crossing that brook and climbing out of the valley led to the Garden of Gethsemane on the shoulders of the Mount of Olives.

After Jesus shared a final supper with His disciples, He led them out of the lighted Upper Room down into the dark Kidron Valley. Carrying no lamp or torch for fear of being seen, they crossed the brook and climbed silently, single file, out of the valley toward Gethsemane. Jesus was deep in thought because He knew what was coming. The disciples were deep in thought because they had no idea what was to come.

We are much like the disciples when we enter dark valleys, not knowing where Jesus is leading us. But having followed Him into the darkness, we would be foolish not to trust Him to lead us out into the light.

THE KIDRON VALLEY, JERUSALEM, ISRAEL
*Jesus would have walked through this valley on His way to the Last
Supper and on His way to pray in the Garden of Gethsemane.*

*When he had finished praying, Jesus left with his disciples and
crossed the Kidron Valley. On the other side there was an olive grove,
and he and his disciples went into it.*

JOHN 18:1 NIV

A Burr on God's Sock

Jesus seems to respond positively to people who won't take no for an answer; who stick to Him like a burr on a sock.

Once when He passed near the towns of Tyre and Sidon, a Canaanite woman—a rank pagan—yelled at the top of her voice for the "Lord, Son of David" to cast the demon out of her daughter. Jesus didn't even answer her (not unprecedented for God— Deuteronomy 1:45), and said the bread of healing was only for Israelites. But again she repeated her plea and Jesus said no. Unwilling to give up, she finally got the best of the Master. Jesus must have thrown back His head and laughed out loud at the bold, importunate faith of this Canaanite woman. Would that He could find such faith in Israel—or in His church!

The woman's daughter was healed because she reasoned with God and wouldn't take no for an answer. If there's something you want, be a burr on the sock of God.

Jesus gave in. "Oh, woman, your faith is something else.
What you want is what you get!"
Right then her daughter became well.

Matthew 15:28 MSG

JACOB'S WELL, SYCHAR, SAMARIA (NABLUS, PALESTINE)
In Nablus (the biblical city of Sychar) is the well of Jacob, dug by the patriarch over 3,000 years ago. Here Jesus met the woman from Samaria. This has been considered a holy place from early in the fourth century when a church was built over the well. The water is as fresh and clear today as in Jesus' day.

"Sir," the woman said,

"I can see that you are a prophet."

JOHN 4:19 NIV

Jesus and Your Mail

It's a little unnerving when someone reads your mail—literally or figuratively. The latter may not happen a lot today, but in the Bible it wasn't that unusual. It was part of a true prophet's job description—to speak things he had no way of knowing other than what God had told him (Amos 3:7).

When Jesus encountered a Samaritan woman at a well, she was holding her own in the conversation until Jesus began reading her mail. He mentioned to her that He knew she wasn't married (which was true) and that she had been married five times previously (which was also true). At that point, she did what anybody might do whose life had just been put up on a giant screen. She paid Him a nervous compliment: "Sir, I can see that you are a prophet." While Jesus' prophetic abilities were astounding, what is even more amazing is that He didn't hold any of her sins against her. He offered her living water—the chance to have all her sins washed away and to live forever.

Whether you realize it or not, Jesus reads your mail every day—and He never loves you any less.

Immovable Forever

Those who trust in the LORD
are as secure as Mount Zion;
They will not be defeated but will endure forever.
Just as the mountains surround and protect Jerusalem,
so the LORD surrounds and protects his people,
both now and forever.

PSALM 125:1-2 NLT

—◦❦◦—

In modern terms, the most widely used synonym for "solid" is Gibraltar: "Solid as the Rock of Gibraltar." The massive, rocky mount on the southern tip of Spain has for centuries been the symbol of stability, endurance, and immovability.

The Gibraltar in the biblical world was Mount Zion. Seemingly impregnable, it was captured from the Jebusites by King David who turned it into the city of God, later named Jerusalem. Zion was guarded by valleys, ringed by mountains, and fed by a life-giving spring of clear water that still flows. Though Zion's structures have fallen scores of times to armies since David claimed it, the mount itself is unmoved.

As the pilgrims made their way to Jerusalem for feasts three times each year, they would look up as they ascended to the city and take heart in the permanence of Zion. For them, to see God's mountain was to see God Himself. As the mountains guarded Zion, so God guarded them. Let their assurance be yours today.

MT. ZION, JERUSALEM

Does the snow ever melt high up in the mountains of Lebanon?
Do the cold, flowing streams from the crags of
Mount Hermon ever run dry?

JEREMIAH 18:14 NLT

Mount Hermon is one of two mountains thought to be the location of Jesus' transfiguration.

As Dependable as Hermon

Spirituality in the days of Jeremiah the prophet was inconsistent. One year the people were worshipping God, the next year they weren't. No prophet could set his clock by the timeliness of worship attendance in Jerusalem.

But there was something predictable in Israel in those days—the life-giving snows on Mount Hermon in Lebanon. The winter-white meant spring-green throughout the whole land. When the snow melted on the three 9,000-foot summits, the runoff seeped into the cracks in the rocks, appearing further below as springs. The springs fed streams and the streams fed the Jordan River, the artery of life for the nation. This predictable cycle stood in stark contrast to the unpredictability of God's own people.

What if God used you as a benchmark for spiritual faithfulness like He did the snows of Hermon? Could He write, "Does my servant (your name) ever fail to obey Me, to worship Me, or to serve Me? Does my servant ever fail to share living water with those in need of Me?" Strive to be as dependable as Mount Hermon.

How Tools Choose

The woodworker draws up plans for his no-god,
traces it on a block of wood.
He shapes it with chisels and planes into human shape —
a beautiful woman, a handsome man,
ready to be placed in a chapel.

ISAIAH 44:13 MSG

Tools are amoral—no consciousness, no will, no joy, no regret. Their will and choice are given to them by the craftsman who wields them. The same kinds of tools that built Auschwitz built St. Paul's Cathedral. The difference in the buildings was the difference between Adolf Hitler and Sir Christopher Wren.

While not necessarily a mason, carpenter, or ironworker, every person is a builder nonetheless—a builder of a life. And every person has tools: gifts and abilities of varying sorts and degrees. To sum it up, every person has time, talent, and treasure that are used each day to craft a life. Every morning, our skills are a little sharper than the day before.

God has created you with care, and in turn, you can use your tools to create your best life possible.

CARPENTRY TOOLS, NAZARETH VILLAGE, NAZARETH, ISRAEL

The Balance of Life

The harvest of the grape vines is finished in the fall and the vines lay dormant in the winter. Before the vines are allowed to begin budding in the spring, they must be pruned—a radical cutting that slices off what has been fruitful in the past in order that it might bear more fruit in the future.

At the same time the woody branches are being cut from the vine and thrown into the fire, the land explodes like a kaleidoscope of color. Reds, yellows, purples, and greens signal the passing of winter and the arrival of spring. Pruning and blooming, cutting and blooming, burning and blooming. That both these passages occur together is a picture of life itself.

In one field of our life, pruning is underway. God is cutting back that which was sufficient yesterday but will be inadequate tomorrow. While in another field, He is causing color, fragrance, and beauty to awaken. There is a balance to life that only God can orchestrate.

The flowers have already appeared in the land;

The time has arrived for pruning the vines,

And the voice of the turtledove has been heard in our land.

Song of Solomon 2:12 NASB

Searching for You

*"They were scattered for lack of a shepherd,
and they became food for every beast of the field and were
scattered."*

EZEKIEL 34:5 NASB

God delivered a long and strong condemnation of the shepherds of Israel—prophets, priests, and princes—through His prophet Ezekiel. They had let the children of Israel wander like lost sheep over the spiritual landscape where they were fair game for any idol-worshiping pagan nation.

Sheep wander away for a variety of reasons: hunger, rebellion, confusion, and temptation. But it's not the reason that matters to God as much as the consequences: A sheep that is wandering alone is an item on the menu for a ravenous beast (1 Peter 5:8). Unlike the shepherds of Israel, Jesus was willing to leave the ninety-nine who were safe in the pen to go into the night and find the one who had wandered away.

If you have wandered away from God, you are being looked for. It doesn't matter to God why you are not where you are supposed to be, it only matters that you are found. If you know you are lost, turn around. The face of the Good Shepherd is the first face you'll see.

MOSAIC, INTERIOR OF THE BASILICA
OF THE TRANSFIGURATION, MT. TABOR, ISRAEL

*Mary, Joseph, and Jesus would have
passed near these pyramids as they
came from Old Cairo.*

Remember

Every parent has played "Twenty Questions" with his or her child. But who, what, when, where, why, and how are more than just questions. They are mile markers on the road of life. They are the way we remember the high and low points, and most especially, the way God sees us through.

When the Israelites left Egypt, Moses gave the fathers instructions on how to remember the day they left slavery behind and how to explain to their children what God did. Before the day of libraries and hard drives, memories were stored in the minds of those who made them, and history was passed down from one generation to the next through stories. The Israelites were destined to fight fierce battles before settling in the Promised Land. How would they know God would give them victory? By remembering what He did for them in Egypt.

The only way to be confident that God will be there for you today is to remember all the times He's been there for you in the past.

"And in the future, your children will ask you,'
What does all this mean?'
Then you will tell them, 'With mighty power the LORD
brought us out of Egypt from our slavery.'"

EXODUS 13:14 NLT

And I saw the holy city—the New Jerusalem—
descending out of heaven from God,
made ready like a bride adorned for her husband.

REVELATION 21:2 NET

The Gates Will Close

To stand on the Mount of Olives overlooking Jerusalem is to view the crossroads of world history. The city has changed hands scores of times as Jews and Arabs, and even Christians, spilled their blood for the right to possess her.

But as important as Jerusalem is—her earthly history is not yet complete—God Himself will one day close her gates forever. There will be a new Jerusalem in which the redeemed of God will dwell forever. In that Jerusalem, what is true now in Christ will be true then in the streets: There will be no Jew, Gentile, Arab or other; no free or slave; no rich or poor. The New Jerusalem will return the human race to the Garden of Eden's sinless perfection: the rule of God and the responsibility of man.

The New Jerusalem's gates are open now, though they will not always be. All who have drunk of the living water that is Christ may enter in by faith now and in person in the future.

Simpler May Be Better

He has told you, O man, what is good;
And what does the LORD require of you
But to do justice, to love kindness,
And to walk humbly with your God?

When Mary and Joseph welcomed baby Jesus into the world, it was supposedly in a simple stable. Visit that spot in Bethlehem today and you'll discover a huge complex of buildings on the traditional site—the Church of the Nativity. Constantine the First ordered that the church be built in A.D. 325 and it has been expanded over the years. Today it is a heavily ornamented edifice, mutually controlled by the Greek Orthodox and Roman Catholic churches.

Ask the average pilgrim which they would rather see today and most would vote for the original stable over the church.

Do we lose something of God's own grandeur—the kind evident in His simple, unadorned style—when we try to make life bigger, better, and grander? Simple things—justice, faithfulness, obedience—are usually enough for God, but usually not for us. At the very least, we ought to ask whether we're doing what we know God wants before doing what we think He prefers.

THE CHURCH OF THE NATIVITY, BETHLEHEM, PALESTINE

*For as the lightning comes from the east and flashes as far as the west,
so will be the coming of the Son of Man.*

MATTHEW 24:27 HCSB

Jesus Will Be Like Lightning

When we say, "Everything from A to Z," we're doing what Jesus did in Matthew 24:27. Jesus used the common Hebrew figure of speech called merism to refer to "everywhere" by saying "from east to west—and everywhere in between." Psalm 139 uses it several times to make the point that God is everywhere (verses 7-9).

What percent of the world's population knew about Jesus' first coming? How many more were aware of His three years of ministry? In both cases, the number was miniscule compared to the world's population.

Just as there is no one in Jerusalem who doesn't see the lightning when it streaks across the sky, so there will not be anyone in the world who doesn't see Jesus' Second Coming in the heavens. It will be daytime on one side of the globe, nighttime on the other. No matter. Wherever east meets west, everyone in that giant circle will see Jesus when He returns.

The question is, How will those who see Him respond? How will you respond?

Don't Expect a Rainbow

When Satan took Jesus up to a high mountain and offered Him the kingdoms of this world, it was likely a tempting sight: Egypt to the southwest, Arabia to the southeast, Mesopotamia to the east, Syria to the north, the regions of Asia Minor to the northwest. And those were just the kingdoms that were known in Jesus' day. After all, temptations aren't legitimate if they aren't tempting.

There's no record in Scripture that at the moment of the offer, a rainbow appeared on the horizon. (There's no record that one didn't, either.) But something gave Jesus hope and strength in that moment to turn down Satan's offer—and resist the other two tests as well (Matthew 4:1-11). And it wasn't just because He was God. The Bible says He was tempted "as we are"—which means He felt the pull, just like we do (Hebrews 2:18; 4:15).

Don't count on a rainbow appearing when you're tempted. But if using the sword of God's Word worked for Jesus, it will likely work for you.

VIEW FROM THE MOUNT OF TEMPTATION, JERICHO, PALESTINE

This is called the Mount of Temptation, thought to be where Satan took Jesus and showed Him the kingdoms of the world.

No temptation has overtaken you

but such as is common to man; and God is faithful,

who will not allow you to be tempted beyond what you are able,

but with the temptation will provide the way of escape also,

so that you will be able to endure it.

1 CORINTHIANS 10:13 NASB

Wrong Answer

"Go," He told him, "wash in the pool of Siloam"
(which means "Sent").
So he left, washed, and came back seeing.

JOHN 9:7 HCSB

When Jesus restored the sight of a man blind since birth, He spat on the ground and put some mud on the man's eyes. He then sent the man to the pool of Siloam to wash off the clay, after which he could see. Another time Jesus put His spit on a blind man's eyes, laid His hands on him, and asked him if he saw anything. The man said, "Sort of." Jesus laid hands on him and prayed again, the man blinked a few times, and voilà!—he could see.

Why didn't Jesus just heal these men instantly like He healed others? We don't know. What's more important is whether it's okay for Jesus to break the rules—to do things in our lives that are outside the lines or not what we expected. If we had been the second man whose vision was fuzzy, we might have said, "Jesus, just do what you normally do. Stop messin' around!" Wrong answer.

Don't ask Jesus for help unless you're willing for Him to give it the way He wants to.

THE POOL OF SILOAM, JERUSALEM, ISRAEL
At the Pool of Siloam, Jesus healed a man born blind.

*Magdala, the birthplace of Mary Magdalene,
is the area where Jesus met her and delivered
her from seven evil spirits.*

No Close Calls

Those opposed to Jesus and His message tried to kill Him on more than one occasion. Once, near Nazareth, they tried to throw Him off a cliff (Luke 4:29). Another time in the temple in Jerusalem, they picked up stones to stone Him (John 8:59). Both times He managed to slip away, the Gospel writers giving cryptic descriptions of His escapes.

The reason Jesus was never entrapped and put to death by His enemies prior to Calvary was because it wasn't His time. The apostle Peter told a huge crowd of Jews at Pentecost that Jesus was "handed over to you by God's set purpose and foreknowledge." That means that no one "caught" Jesus and put Him to death. It means He handed Himself over to His enemies because it was finally time.

Psalm 139:16 says, "All the days ordained for me were written in your book before one of them came to be." There are no "close calls" in God's plan—only days laid out for you like they were laid out for Jesus.

This man was handed over to you
by God's set purpose and foreknowledge;
and you, with the help of wicked men,
put him to death by nailing him to the cross.

ACTS 2:23 NIV

Learning Obedience

Though he was God's Son,
he learned trusting-obedience
by what he suffered, just as we do.

HEBREWS 5:8 MSG

When a parent chooses to test a child's obedience by sending him to the refrigerator to get an ice cream bar, that's known in the parenting business as being unclear on the concept of obedience. There is no test of obedience when we do something we want to do. Obedience is only proven when we carry out something that we, given the choice, would rather not have been asked to do.

Some people are surprised—amazed, even—when they consider that Jesus had to learn obedience. He learned it the same way we do—by the path of suffering. It may be suffering a little (obeying the speed limit) or suffering a lot (dying on a cross). Regardless of the degree, suffering is the universal prerequisite for learning obedience.

Jesus even asked His Father to let the cup of suffering He was about to drink pass Him by. When He was handed it anyway, He mingled His tears with the cup and drank it out of trust and obedience.

How much would you be willing to suffer to learn obedience?

THE BASILICA OF THE AGONY, JERUSALEM, ISRAEL
This church in the Garden of Gethsemane is believed to be where Jesus prayed fervently. The rock in the foreground, called the Rock of the Agony, is thought to be the exact spot where He prayed.

THE WAILING WALL, THE TEMPLE MOUNT, JERUSALEM, ISRAEL

A single day in your courts
is better than a thousand anywhere else!
I would rather be a gatekeeper in the house of my God
than live the good life in the homes of the wicked.

PSALM 84:10 NLT

Favorite Place to Be

A woman on an airplane was shocked when a famous celebrity took the seat next to her. Noting her obvious surprise, he said, "Well, everybody has to be somewhere."

While that's true, there's a difference between "has to be" and "want to be." Most of the places we "are" in our life are obligatory. We have to go to work, we have to go to meetings, we have to spend time with our family. And we don't mind those obligations. But we don't learn as much about a person by learning where they *have* to be as by where they *choose* to be.

The psalmist said that, given the choice, he'd rather spend one day in God's house than a thousand elsewhere. The New Testament reply is not that we'd rather spend a day in church than a thousand anywhere else. It's that we'd *choose* to acknowledge—for a minute, an hour, even a day—the God who lives not in a temple but in our heart.

He can be our favorite place to be. The choice is ours.

But He replied to them, "When it is evening, you say,
'It will be fair weather, for the sky is red.'
And in the morning, 'There will be a storm today,
for the sky is red and threatening.' Do you know how to discern
the appearance of the sky, but cannot discern the signs of the times?"

MATTHEW 16:2–3 NASB

Jesus would have seen this area when He was down in the Jericho region.

Pale by Comparison

"Red sky in the morning, sailors take warning. Red sky at night, sailors delight." Since storm clouds in Israel move from west to east, a red sky in the morning means storms approaching; red sky in the evening means storms are past.

Such proverbial wisdom isn't foolproof, but eons of observation have proved it right more often than not. Granted, watching events for several thousand years provides more data than one generation of Jesus' ministry. Still, the spiritual changes were so dramatic in His day that He accused the religious leaders of being insensitive—of lacking the powers of observation and discernment.

We might be guilty of the same—being more aware of trends in fashion, food, and fun, than in the way critical pieces are moving on the chessboard of this world, aligning themselves in accord with the larger purposes of God.

Read your Bible. Look at the world. Pray for discernment. It may be that food, fashion, and fun will pale by comparison to what you see.

The Opposite of Faith

Jesus reprimanded them. "Why are you such cowards,
such faint-hearts?" Then he stood up and told the wind
to be silent, the sea to quiet down:
"Silence!" The sea became smooth as glass.

MATTHEW 8:26 MSG

—◦⋄◦—

Ask most people what the opposite of faith is and they will offer something in the semantic range of "doubt:" unbelief, disbelief, skepticism, or cynicism. But for Jesus, the opposite of faith is fear.

Jesus and His disciples were crossing the Sea of Galilee when a dangerous storm arose. The disciples were panicked since Jesus was taking a nap. When they woke Him He didn't say, "Why do you disbelieve?" He said, "Why are you afraid, you men of little faith?" We tend to think of courage being the opposite of fear, but Jesus juxtaposed faith and fear.

Faith and fear are both perspectives on the future—the future being the next five minutes or the next five years. It is easy to face the future with fear—think of all the things that could happen: loss of money, health, friends, employment, purpose, peace, or place in life. That's what the disciples were feeling. For them, the future looked bleak. Therefore, they had fear, not faith.

Having faith doesn't mean having religion. It means factoring in Jesus' presence when you contemplate the future.

SUNRISE OVER THE SEA OF GALILEE FROM TIBERIAS, ISRAEL

Ask for a Miracle

Jesus turning water into wine at the wedding at Cana sounds suspiciously like what the devil asked Him to do in the wilderness: turn a stone into bread (Matthew 4:3). Jesus did the miracle at Cana but refused the one in the desert.

The difference was one of need. At the wedding, a time of celebration in which wine played a customary role, a miracle was needed. In the wilderness, the offer had an evil motive: to get Jesus to show off.

That distinction doesn't mean that every time we have a need Jesus is going to work a miracle. (There were lots of legitimate needs Jesus didn't address during His ministry on earth. For whatever reason, the same appears to be true of His ministry while in heaven.) But it does put our legitimate needs in the same category as the legitimate need in Cana. In other words, it doesn't hurt to ask for a miracle.

We forget that Jesus was the God-*Man*. Human needs were important to Him then, just as they are now. Don't be afraid to ask.

The wine supply ran out during the festivities,

so Jesus' mother spoke to him about the problem.

"They have no more wine," she told him.

JOHN 2:3 NLT

Bearing the Patibulum

As they were on the way,
they came across a man named Simon,
who was from Cyrene,
and they forced him to carry Jesus' cross.

MATTHEW 27:32 NLT

A peculiar concept (at first glance) in the New Testament is the idea that we participate in the sufferings of Christ (Romans 8:17; Philippians 3:10; 1 Peter 4:13). Even more peculiar is the idea that we make up "what is lacking in the sufferings of Christ" (Colossians 1:24 NET).

We might have asked a man named Simon about participating in such sufferings. He was pulled from the crowd by Roman soldiers to carry the heavy crosspiece, the *patibulum,* of Christ's cross on the way to Calvary. He knew something, literally, of participating in the sufferings of Christ. Simon added nothing to the spiritual meaning of Christ's suffering—atonement and reconciliation. But he did participate in another way. When he bore the *patibulum,* he bore the shame as well, even though involuntarily. When we voluntarily identify with Christ, we likewise bear the shame of One rejected by the world.

There is fellowship in such suffering, and fellowship means oneness. Suffering is one way we become one with Christ.

SIMON OF CYRENE HELPS CARRY THE CROSS OF JESUS,
VIA DOLOROSA, JERUSALEM

The Two-Way Gate

Then the glory of the LORD departed from the
threshold of the temple and stood over the cherubim . . . .
and they stood at the door of the east gate of the LORD's
house, and the glory of the God of Israel was above them.

EZEKIEL 10:18–19 NKJV

It behooves us to remember that God has thrown up His hands at times and walked out of the meeting. He did it when He flooded the earth in Genesis. Jesus did it when He tore a strip off the Pharisees for their hypocrisy (Matthew 23) and when He broke up their shopping mall (Matthew 21:12).

God isn't impulsive. Rather, as the Bible says, He is longsuffering. Indeed, it is His goodness and longsuffering that should lead us to repentance (Romans 2:4). But if we persist, God does have limits. In the Old Testament, He left His meeting-place with Israel, the temple. His glory rose out of the temple in the presence of angels and just left—departed by way of the east gate of the temple complex. By the same gate He promised to return (Ezekiel 43:1-9). But that doesn't make His leaving any less real for those who watched Him go.

Can you imagine anything more terrible than the sight of God's back as He leaves? May His goodness and longsuffering lead us to repentance.

THE EASTERN GATES, JERUSALEM, ISRAEL
The Bible says that Christ will return at this location. These Eastern Gates to Jerusalem will open when the time is right to receive the King of kings, Jesus Christ, the Son of God.

Sweet Sorrow

All tears are salty, but not all tears are bitter. Take separation from a loved one, for instance. Leaving someone we love may produce tears, but they won't be bitter if we leave on good terms—and especially if we leave with the expectation of seeing them again.

Jesus left His disciples twice—once when He was crucified and again when He ascended into heaven. The first time, the disciples were frustrated, fearful, despairing, and even angry. They had missed the part of Jesus' teaching about being raised from the dead (John 2:19), so they were totally confused. The One who carried all their hopes for the future had suddenly been taken away.

The second time Jesus left, it was a different story. He was very much alive, at peace, and communicating with them. After ascending into heaven, two "white-robed men" appeared and told them not to worry. Jesus would be returning. Instead of dispersing in despair like the first time, they joined together in prayer and celebration.

Parting is a sweet sorrow when it's only temporary. Come quickly, Lord Jesus.

INTERIOR OF THE CHURCH OF THE PRIMACY OF ST. PETER,
SEA OF GALILEE, ISRAEL

The rock shelf in the foreground is called the Mensa Christi *("Christ's Table")
and is believed to be the rock shelf on which Jesus had breakfast with His disciples.*

*It was not long after he said this
that he was taken up into the sky while they were watching,
and he disappeared into a cloud.*

ACTS 1:9 NLT

Fearless Fishing

Jesus called out to them, "Come, be my disciples, and I will show you how to fish for people!"

MATTHEW 4:19 NLT

Mention "witnessing" to the average Christian and fear is the normal response. Compare that fear with a typical scene of a fisherman in a boat on a quiet lake, standing in a rushing mountain stream, or dozing with a cane pole by a farm pond. Witnessing is stressful; fishing is stress-relieving. The contrast is heightened by Jesus using fishing as an illustration for witnessing. Did He mean to suggest witnessing should be as relaxing as fishing?

What if the fisherman was responsible for talking face-to-face with the fish and convincing him to hop in the boat or creel? That's how we sometimes feel about witnessing. But Jesus used the illustration of fishing in order to deemphasize our responsibility. All we do is cast the net or the lure. Fishing, in the strict sense, is the act of trying to get fish by any means. We can return home with no fish and still say we "went fishing."

In the same way, witnessing is a matter of making it possible for men and women to come to Jesus. We cast the net and leave the results to God.

FISHERMEN FISHING FROM A BOAT,
SEA OF GALILEE, ISRAEL *(left)*

Second Fiddle

We see it every time there's a beauty pageant. The runners-up are announced and applauded until only two contestants remain. As soon as the winner is announced, the second runner-up may as well fall through a trap door and disappear. No one gets less attention than the one who comes in second.

That's a recipe for disappointment at best, envy and jealousy at worse. What was it about Elizabeth, then, the relative of Mary, that made her so blessedly content to be chosen as the mother of John the Baptist instead of Jesus? Yes, she was older and perhaps wiser (Luke 1:18). But she was aware that Mary's son would be Lord, not hers. Yet she still counted her place in God's plan as an honor and a blessing. In time, she even conveyed her attitude to her son. John recognized his destiny was to grow smaller while Jesus grew larger (John 3:30).

It's not easy for fallen human nature to be content with playing second fiddle. But it helps to remember that God assigns the positions (1 Corinthians 12:11, 18) and then rewards them on the same basis: faithfulness.

"*What an honor this is,*
that the mother of my Lord should visit me!"

LUKE 1:43 NLT

THE MOUNT OF TEMPTATION, NEAR JERICHO, PALESTINE

*Again, the devil took Him to a very high mountain
and showed Him all the kingdoms of the world and their glory;
and he said to Him, "All these things I will give You,
if You fall down and worship me."*

MATTHEW 4:8–9 NASB

Qualified to Help

It is not easy today being the keeper of the eye-gate. Through that gate passes light waves reflected off the bangles and baubles of this world—stuff we would die to have. We see the lifestyles of the rich, the lifestyles of the famous, and the lifestyles of the rich *and* famous. And we want that life to be our own. "Why did I get my life and they got theirs?" we wonder—all too seriously.

But when we pray and ask Jesus to give us the grace of contentment—remembering that He, too, was tempted like we are (Hebrews 2:18; 4:15)—we forget the most important part. He was tempted *way* beyond what we are.

The devil took Jesus up to a high mountain and offered Him the whole world. It was his to give (1 John 5:19): the kingdoms, the power, the glory, the riches and the fame—all of it. But Jesus turned down the offer in order to pursue the will of God for His life.

Because He knows what His temptation felt like, He's qualified to help us with ours.

Raising the Bar

"Woe to you experts in the law, because you have taken away the key to knowledge.
You yourselves have not entered, and you have hindered those who were entering."

LUKE 11:52 NIV

—◦◦✝◦◦—

Putting Jesus and lawyers (experts on the Old Testament law) in the same room together was not a good idea—much like mixing oil and water. There was just something about those men that got under His skin. It seems as if Jesus held them responsible for the lack of faith and spiritual perception He found in Israel. Not only did these resident theologians not recognize who He was, they were like spiritual blinders on the populace as a whole.

In another place, Jesus said it would be better to be thrown into the sea with a millstone tied around your neck than to block the spiritual light of another person or to lead them astray (Luke 17:2). And it wasn't just a first-century problem. Nowadays, it's easy for someone to make a cynic out of a wide-eyed, bushy-tailed new believer by running down the church and her leaders. It's easier to criticize than to be constructive.

Jesus takes exception to such practice and so should we.

She came up behind Jesus and touched the fringe of his robe.
Immediately, the bleeding stopped.

LUKE 8:44 NLT

Taking Jesus to the Mall

Sometimes it's hard to imagine Jesus doing the same everyday things we do—but He did. He went from people's houses to the marketplace to other nearby cities, rubbing shoulders with the masses. If Hollywood was typecasting God for a major production, Jesus wouldn't have been given a call-back. He was far too much of a commoner.

But it was His very availability that put Him in touch with the people He came to save. Once, in a crowded street or marketplace, the press of people was so great that He suddenly felt healing power leave His body. Discovering a woman had reached out in faith to touch the edge of His robe, He pronounced her healed. *That's* why Jesus spent time in the streets—because that's where the people were who needed Him.

Is it so different today? The people with needs are definitely still there, but one thing might be missing: Jesus. Today, Jesus' primary way of ministering to people is through our lives and our relationships with others. It's a whole new reason to go to the mall.

Just Generosity

Doom to you who buy up all the houses and
grab all the land for yourselves—
Evicting the old owners, posting no trespassing signs,
Taking over the country,
leaving everyone homeless and landless.

ISAIAH 5:8 MSG

In ancient Israel, land was not to be sold, only leased. Moses had assigned the land to tribes and clans and it was to remain in the families as a perpetual inheritance. In due time, however, the prophets' railed against the social injustice that found the wealthy buying up fields and joining house to house. Not only were they "turning paradise into parking lots," they were taking away the source of income of the lower class: their land and the fruits thereof.

God is serious about social justice. Unfortunately, it cannot be engineered as Marx thought, nor does capitalism ensure it as our founding fathers hoped. Instead, social justice flows from only one source: our hearts. When people realize how generous God was toward them (after all, He gave up the life of His own Son), they start becoming more generous toward others. They stop with the profit-at-all-costs attitude. They still do things that are profitable, but they do as much for others as for themselves.

The generosity we have toward others is a measure of how generous we think God has been toward us.

SUNSET OVER NAZARETH, ISRAEL

Promise Keepers

"Whenever the rainbow appears in the clouds,
I will see it and remember the everlasting covenant
between God and all living creatures
of every kind on the earth."

GENESIS 9:16 NIV

Albert Schweitzer was a French theologian and medical doctor. He won the 1952 Nobel Peace Prize for his humanitarian work at a missionary hospital in Africa. As a man of many disciplines, he spent years searching for a unifying theme for all his work. He found it in "reverence for life."

That's not a bad life-statement for anyone, but for a biblical theologian it's especially appropriate. After the Flood in Noah's day, God made a covenant with all living beings on the earth that He would never again take the life of all living creatures by such a flood of water. And He put the rainbow in the heavens to mark the making of the promise.

If God has such a deep reverence for life, shouldn't His people? Do we tread as lightly as we should on this planet when it comes to other living beings besides ourselves—human and non-human? Yes, we're in charge (Genesis 1:26). But practically speaking, Schweitzer had it right: We should have a reverence for all life.

More Than Enough

There may not be a more frequently-used qualifier in the human language than "only." Dictionaries say it means "and nothing more." "We have five loaves and two fish," the disciples said to Jesus. "That's it. These and nothing more." When it comes to doing something bigger than our resources (paying a medical bill, starting a business, sending a child to school, going on a vacation) "only" is a limiter; "only" means we don't have enough.

That was definitely the case when there were five to ten thousand people who needed food, and the disciples could only round up five loaves and two fish. It looked like the meal wasn't going to happen. That's when Jesus said what He always says (maybe not out loud) when the need is greater than the human resources: "Bring them here to Me." We know the story—there was more left over after the meal than what they had to begin with.

If you are facing a need bigger than you are, imagine Jesus saying, "Bring what you have to Me." He can make it become more than enough.

And they said to Him, "We have here only five loaves and two fish."
He said, "Bring them here to Me."

Jesus' baptism site, Jordan River, Kasr El Yehud, Israel
In Jesus' day, the Jordan River was wider and had a greater flow of water.

And a voice from heaven said, "This is my Son,
whom I love; with him I am well pleased."

MATTHEW 3:17 NIV

Forewarned, Forearmed

To a modern child, what Jesus' Father did to Him might seem a little inconsistent. But it shouldn't have seemed inconsistent to any discerning Israelite.

It was time for Jesus' public ministry to begin. His cousin, John the Baptist, was baptizing repentant Jews in the Jordan River, a way of renewing their "baptism" in the Red Sea when God redeemed their ancestors from slavery in Egypt; a way to say, "I'm ready to renew my relationship with God." Just as Moses went into the Red Sea, Jesus went into the Jordan to be baptized by John. And just as Israel's next stop was the Sinai wilderness where their commitment to God was tested, so immediately after His baptism was Jesus led by the Spirit into the Judean wilderness to have His own commitment tested by the devil (Matthew 4:1).

Would a loving father profess his pleasure with his son and then send him immediately to boot camp in the desert? Apparently so. And because God did it with Jesus, He might allow us to be tested the same way. Forewarned is forearmed.

Footprints in the Stone

The soldiers led Jesus away into the palace . . .
put a purple robe on him . . . twisted together a
crown of thorns . . . struck him on the head . . .
spit on him . . . paid homage to him . . . .
Then they led him out to crucify him.

MARK 15:16–20 NIV

Jerusalem has been ravaged and rebuilt so many times since Jesus' day that most locations related to His life are only approximations. But one sight that is universally accepted as genuine is the stone pavement in the Roman military complex near the temple.

On this pavement, Jesus stood and was humiliated and beaten by Roman soldiers before being led out to die on Calvary. On these stones, Jesus' blood and sweat fell in a divine display of human suffering. On these stones, the very worst and best of humanity came face to face.

Of all the sites of antiquity to be the best-preserved, it would have to be this one—the one that makes us want to turn away. Peering at the ancient pavement, we look for our own footprints, knowing we were there that day in the loins of our Roman cousins. Time may have washed away the evidence of our presence, but only God can wash clean our souls for what we did.

JESUS TAKES UP HIS CROSS, THE LITHOSTROTOS, JERUSALEM
This paving is in the courtyard of the Antonia Fortress.
On this pavement Jesus took up His cross and began His grueling trek to His crucifixion.

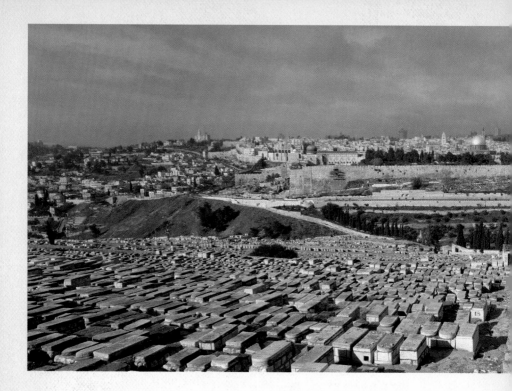

"*Let the nations be roused;*
let them advance into the Valley of Jehoshaphat,
for there I will sit to judge all the nations on every side."

JOEL 3:12 NIV

No Fear of Judgment

Today, the western flank of the Mount of Olives, overlooking Jerusalem, is covered by thousands of Jewish graves. Descending down that mountainside leads to the Kidron Valley, the ravine separating the Mount and Jerusalem, also assigned another name by tradition: the Valley of Jehoshaphat.

Jehoshaphat means "the Lord judges," and the valley gets its name from references in the Book of Joel (vv. 3:2, 12). The Valley of Jehoshaphat is the place where God's great, final judgment is to take place. As tradition began to identify the Kidron Valley as the Valley of Jehoshaphat, Jews began to be buried on the hills surrounding the valley to ensure not being overlooked when the resurrection occurs and judgment takes place.

With faith in Christ comes the assurance that "there is now no condemnation for those who are in Christ Jesus" (Romans 8:1); no need to fear being missed, or excluded, at the end of the age. How wonderful that Christ was judged in our place; that He suffered so we might live free of the fear of death and judgment.

Reason with Jesus

As they approached the village gate,
they met a funeral procession —
a woman's only son was being carried out for burial.
And the mother was a widow.

LUKE 7:12 MSG

It's clear that Jesus did not heal everyone who was sick, or resuscitate every dead person during His earthly ministry. That fact immediately raises the question, How did He choose? Did God direct Him? (John 5:30; 14:10) If so, how did God choose?

By keeping the event in the realm of Jesus' humanity, it's easier to reckon with a thorny problem. A woman, a widow, has lost her only son who, in that culture, was possibly her only means for future, if not present, support. Jesus encounters the funeral procession leaving the village of Nain and is struck with compassion—just like we might be.

This young man had not died "in full vigor, like sheaves gathered in season (Job 5:26). He died early—before His time (Jesus called him a "young man"). Yes, death is abnormal in itself. But an early death may have even raised Jesus' ire at the devil who uses death as a means of instilling fear (Hebrews 2:14-15). That was enough—this young man would rejoin his mother.

Jesus is not arbitrary. He understands the humanity of our suffering. Talk with Him about your needs.

EXTERIOR OF NAIN CHURCH, ISRAEL
This church was erected on the traditional site where Jesus healed the widow's son.

The Rule for Rules

Old Testament, New Testament. Law, Grace. Works, Freedom. We're two thousand years past the transition from the former to the latter and we still get confused. Think how it must have been for those alive when it happened.

Jesus and His disciples were walking through a grain field on the Sabbath. The disciples broke off some grains of wheat to munch on as they walked and the ever-vigilant Rules Police, the Pharisees, called them to account. It was against the law of Moses to harvest wheat on the Sabbath. Instead of saying, "Give me a break," which we might have done, Jesus explained how even in the Old Testament the King of Israel did the same thing one day, meaning that the Sabbath was not more important than people. If someone needed help on the Sabbath, it was totally appropriate to help them.

The apostle Paul said something similar in Romans 14:17 when he spoke about how the kingdom of God is not about rules, but about goodness, peace, and joy in the Holy Spirit. Keep that in mind as you work out your salvation.

Then he said to them, "The Sabbath was made to benefit people,
and not people to benefit the Sabbath."

MARK 2:27 NLT

Jesus lived in Capernaum for a time and used it as his base. From this place he traveled throughout Galilee. Jesus also taught in a synagogue in Capernaum.

How to Amaze Jesus

In the eyes of the Jews, Roman soldiers (Gentiles) were dogs. So when Jesus entered Capernaum it probably seemed unusual for a group of Jewish elders to approach Him on behalf of a local Roman centurion whose servant was sick. But this was apparently no ordinary Roman officer. In the first place, he was a compassionate man, concerned about the welfare of his servant. And second, he was a generous and conciliatory man, having built the Jewish community a new synagogue.

Apparently those qualities struck Jesus, for He left immediately to go and heal the man's servant. But then the clincher came: He discovered the Roman soldier understood the notion of authority. The centurion and the Savior were both authorities in their separate domains. All either had to do to get things accomplished (build a synagogue or heal a servant) was give the word and it was done. Jesus was amazed at this kind of understanding and faith.

If you want to amaze Jesus, give Him the opportunity to exercise His authority.

When Jesus heard this, he was amazed at him,
and turning to the crowd following him, he said,
"I tell you, I have not found such great faith even in Israel."

LUKE 7:9 NIV

Hanging in the Balance

*Jesus, full of the Holy Spirit, returned from the Jordan
and was led by the Spirit in the desert,
where for forty days he was tempted by the devil.*

LUKE 4:1-2 NIV

It's hard to say that anything in the New Testament is more important than the death and resurrection of Jesus. But an encounter at the beginning of His ministry was a watershed event that made everything else possible.

When the devil confronted Jesus, the last Adam (1 Corinthians 15:45), in the wilderness, he was replaying his encounter with the first Adam in the Garden of Eden. After all, Jesus was the only sinless human on earth since Adam, and Satan thought the encounter would be just as predictable. Satan took down sinless Adam, so sinless Jesus was the next target. Satan probably thought the encounter with Jesus would be easier. Adam was in lush Eden with every need supplied; Jesus was in the burning desert having fasted for forty days. Everything hung in the balance. If Jesus had yielded to Satan's temptations, the cross would never have happened. Thankfully, the last Adam succeeded where the first Adam failed.

Every temptation we face is a micro-drama of the same order. The Adam we emulate yields a victory or defeat for the devil—and for us.

VIEW FROM THE MOUNT OF TEMPTATION, JERICHO, PALESTINE
The Mount of Temptation

THE AQUEDUCT AT CAESAREA, ISRAEL
On returning to Nazareth, Mary, Joseph, and Jesus would have passed this way along the coastal road.

"If you believe in me, come and drink!
For the Scriptures declare that rivers
of living water will flow out from within."

JOHN 7:38 NLT

Spiritual Self-Hydration

When Herod began fortifying the seaport of Caesarea in the first century B.C., fresh water had to be "piped" in from the springs at the base of Mount Carmel, which was ten miles away. The amount of labor—and the engineering finesse—needed to build an aqueduct at a slight decline over ten miles is staggering to consider.

Earlier, King Hezekiah of Judah needed to get a source of fresh water inside the city walls of Jerusalem to protect against siege. His men dug a 1,750-foot tunnel through solid rock so water could flow from the Gihon Spring, outside the walls, to the Pool of Siloam inside. These were huge feats of engineering, all for a drink of life-sustaining water.

It is against the backdrop of the value of water in an arid land that Jesus stood up at the Feast of Tabernacles and said that any person could be spiritually self-hydrating forever. You don't need to stack stones and chisel rock to quench your spiritual thirst. All you must do is believe in Jesus to have access to spiritual hydration.

People in Your Path

What a coincidence! Mary and Joseph were obeying the Mosaic law by presenting their firstborn male son before the Lord at the temple. At the same time, a godly man named Simeon decided to go into the temple courts. Out of all the people milling around in the crowded temple precinct, Simeon looked at the baby Jesus and knew He was the Messiah of Israel. Mary and Joseph were astonished at what Simeon prayed about their baby. Just then, an eighty-four-year-old prophetess named Anna saw the baby and recognized Him as well, prophesying to the people in the temple courts.

These "chance" encounters really weren't by chance at all. The Holy Spirit had led Simeon into the temple at the precise time to intersect with the family. Anna basically lived at the temple, but her prophetic gift allowed her to see who Jesus was.

Do you believe the Holy Spirit is as active in your life as He was in Mary's and Joseph's—putting people in your path to minister to you? Don't sell "chance" encounters short. They are more likely divine appointments.

Moved by the Spirit, he went into the temple courts.
When the parents brought in the child Jesus to
do for him what the custom of the Law required,
Simeon took him in his arms and praised God. . . .

LUKE 2:27-28 NIV

Where Is the Wise Man?

Entering the house, they saw the child with Mary His mother,
and falling to their knees, they worshiped Him.
Then they opened their treasures and presented Him
with gifts: gold, frankincense, and myrrh.

MATTHEW 2:11 HCSB

Among the most mysterious individuals in the Bible are the three magi—the Astronomers, Sages, or perhaps Philosophers—who came to bow down before the baby Jesus in Bethlehem. We know little of them—from whence they came, how they knew about the birth of Jesus, or why they felt compelled to seek Him out.

History and tradition have dubbed them "the wise men" and even concluded there were three based on the number of their gifts. What endears them most to us is what they did when they discovered the newborn King. Even though His parents were commoners instead of royalty ... even though they found Him in a stable instead of a palace ... even though He was surrounded by smelly animals instead of perfumed courtiers, they still fell to their knees and worshiped Him.

The apostle Paul asked, "Where is the wise man? Where is the scholar? Where is the philosopher of this age?" (1 Corinthians 1:20) We know where three of them were—on bended knee worshipping an infant-king.

May God grant such wisdom to us all.

ST. THEODOSIOS MONASTERY, EAST OF BETHLEHEM, PALESTINE
The cave under the raised lights in the foreground is said to be where the wise men
stayed on their way to see Jesus.

What God is Going to Do

"Herod, Herod," we might have said, shaking our head. "Give it up. God's going to do what God's going to do."

It's easy for us to think poorly of Herod's jealousy and rage. But understanding the man is to understand his irrational behavior. By cunning and daring, he climbed the ladder of Roman authority in Palestine. As an Edomite, he was hated by the Jews, but tolerated because he built them a beautiful temple in Jerusalem. Given the blood-letting that went on among politicos, he probably slept with one eye open his entire thirty-four-year reign. When he heard that a promised King of the Jews had been born in Bethlehem, he became enraged and had all the infant boys in the area killed.

Is our fallen human flesh much different than Herod's? Don't we try to self-protect when we think we're losing the advantage? Aren't we tempted to do unto others before they do unto us?

Like Herod, we ought to give it up. God's going to do what God's going to do.

THE ANCIENT BATH HOUSE IN ONE OF HEROD'S PALACES, HERODION, PALESTINE
This is the site of one of Herod's opulent palaces and where he was buried.

When Herod realized that he had been outwitted by the Magi,

he was furious, and he gave orders to kill all the boys in Bethlehem

and its vicinity who were two years old and under, in accordance

with the time he had learned from the Magi.

MATTHEW 2:16 NIV

The Samaritan woman, taken aback, asked, "How come you,
a Jew, are asking me, a Samaritan woman, for a drink?"
(Jews in those days wouldn't be caught dead talking to Samaritans.)

JOHN 4:9 MSG

Amen, Jesus!

When Jesus stopped in Samaria and talked with a woman from the village of Sychar, the tension that developed wasn't for normal reasons. Usually, most Jews and Samaritans got along as well as tail-tied cats and dogs. But Jesus' issues with the woman were moral, not racial, which makes the story a worthy one.

The Samaritans, in the Jews' eyes, were half-breeds. When Assyria conquered the northern tribes of Israel in 722 B.C. they took most of the Jews captive and moved in a large number of their own people—a common practice for conquerors. In time, Assyrians and Jews in the area intermarried (a sin for a Jew). Their descendants were anathema to the self-righteous Jews in Israel—and thus, a racial equivalent of the Grand Canyon separated Judea and Samaria in Jesus' day.

But Jesus made the point that needed to be made: There is only one kind of prejudice acceptable in God's sight, and it's not the racial kind. We can be prejudiced against sin as long as we're accepting of the sinner.

Can Jesus hear an "Amen?"

Moments in Time

Peter blurted out, "Lord, this is wonderful!
If you want me to, I'll make three shrines,
one for you, one for Moses, and one for Elijah."

MATTHEW 17:4 NLT

—◦◦✝◦◦—

Who doesn't love Peter? The man was all energy and ideas. When Jesus took him and James and John up on top of a high mountain, it was for one moment in time—so they could witness His glory. James and John were appropriately silent with awe when Moses and Elijah appeared, but not Peter. His first thought was to build memorials, some kind of permanent structures to which they would return—just the four of them.

We smile at Peter because *we know we might have done the same thing!* Peter is the eight-year-old boy who gets his two best friends and builds a fort in the back yard and puts a sign on it that says, "Members Only!" or "No Girls Allowed!" We love cliques. We love the top of the mountain. And we love hanging out with important people.

But we know that's a fantasy. Life is lived in the valley among the people who are just like us. Don't confuse a mountaintop with life, or a moment in time with time itself.

MOSAIC AT MT. TABOR

He's God and We're Not

*Near the Sheep Gate in Jerusalem there was a pool,
in Hebrew called Bethesda, with five alcoves.
Hundreds of sick people — blind, crippled, paralyzed —
were in these alcoves.*

JOHN 5:2–3 MSG

When President Franklin Roosevelt saw a pond on a tract of land in Maryland, it reminded him of the biblical "pool of Bethesda." It is now the location of the U.S. Navy's primary medical center, Bethesda Naval Hospital.

The pool of Bethesda was Jerusalem's hospital. People crowded the area waiting for an angel to stir up the waters and release healing for those who could get into the pool. Jesus healed a man there who had been an invalid for thirty-eight years. It appears from the record that no one else was healed. Since there was no expression of faith on the man's part, why was he healed? And why did Jesus heal only this one man, leaving all the others with their illness? We could speculate without profit. The truth is, we simply don't know why Jesus did what He did. But this is okay, and it's to be expected, given that He's God and we're not.

We can't expect to understand all of Jesus' actions. But we should maintain faith that God can heal us, no matter what our ailment might be.

THE POOL OF BETHESDA, JERUSALEM, ISRAEL

THE SYNAGOGUE AT KORAZIN, ISRAEL

*The Jews of this once-thriving town refused to allow Jesus to preach there. Jesus warned them
about their disbelief as many mighty works of the Lord had been performed in their vicinity.*

*From everyone who has been given much, much will be demanded;
and from the one who has been entrusted with much,
much more will be asked.*

LUKE 12:48 NIV

Right and Fair

We often hear people say about God and His actions or words, "That's not fair!" And in response, doctrinally-minded folks say, "God's not about fair. He's about what's right!" Such dialogue suggests that if God is going to be right, He can't be fair, and vice versa. But are the two mutually exclusive?

In a parable that Jesus told, He seemed to suggest that right was fair and that God is both. The bottom line in the parable was that people who do the wrong thing because they don't know better will be less accountable than people who know better and still choose the wrong course. That seems right and fair, doesn't it? Jesus illustrated this again with His pronouncements to two cities, Korazin and Bethsaida. Jesus performed many miracles there and the people still didn't believe! They would be held more accountable than the people in Tyre and Sidon who saw no miracles from Jesus at all.

With fairness comes a warning: Better not to hear and see than to hear and see and not believe.

Control Issues

The man Jesus encountered in the region of the Gerasenes was definitely not normal. He had beyond-human strength provided by demons that had invaded his psyche. But in spite of his uniqueness, the way Mark described the man makes him like us in one very important way: *No one was strong enough to control him.*

Who among us can control another person? Who among us can be controlled? Parents try to control their children, spouses try to control each other, and dictators try to control whole populations. But even if we're sitting down in submission on the outside, like the proverbial child we're standing up rebelling or protesting on the inside. We may not be dominated by demons like the man Jesus encountered, but our flesh is out of control nonetheless (Romans 7:14–20). Only an encounter with Jesus can bring us under control.

If you have "control issues," ask Jesus to meet with you and remove them. It's the only way to finally be free—free to live under His control.

Whenever he was put into chains and shackles—as he often was—
he snapped the chains from his wrists and smashed the shackles.
No one was strong enough to control him.

MARK 5:4 NLT

Fight or Flight

The church of Jesus Christ gave itself a black eye during the period from the eleventh to the thirteenth centuries. A dozen or so military campaigns or crusades were launched from Europe to retake Jerusalem and the Holy Land from invading Muslim forces. Countless lives were lost as Christians and Muslims see-sawed back and forth over land and a city important to both religions.

The irony of the whole period is that Jesus said He was not an earthly King; that His Kingdom was not of this world. And He proved it by not calling on His followers, or legions of angels, to take up arms. So how is it that the church drew their swords in the Crusades after Jesus told Peter to sheath his? (John 18:10).

It seems we don't pick our battles the same way Jesus would. We fight over things that Jesus wouldn't—earthly things that have little bearing on His spiritual Kingdom.

The next time you see a fight on the horizon, ask yourself what Jesus would do.

This Crusader fortress is built at the opening to Sidon Harbor. Jesus would have spent some time in this area.

*Then Jesus answered, " I am not an earthly king.
If I were, my followers would have fought when I was arrested by
the Jewish leaders. But my Kingdom is not of this world."*

JOHN 18:36 NLT

You welcome me as a guest,

anointing my head with oil.

PSALM 23:5 NLT

Guests of God

The fundamental condiment of the Middle East was, and still is, olive oil. Ancient, gnarled olive trees dot the rugged landscape from one end of the Mediterranean to the other. The Mediterranean cultures have been tending their wounds, indulging their palates, and welcoming their guests with this fruity, liquid gold since time immemorial.

Shepherds used olive oil to anoint their sheep, putting it on cuts for healing and on heads and faces to keep insects at bay. Thus, when David pictured himself as a sheep belonging to Yahweh, he imagined himself being anointed with oil. But his anointing was also indicative of another use of oil—as an act of personal hospitality; a sign of welcoming.

Instead of using oil, God anointed Jesus with the Holy Spirit (Luke 4:18; Acts 10:38), a welcoming and blessing we may transfer to our own receipt of the Spirit (Romans 8:9, 14-17). What a welcome God gives us into His Kingdom, His house, and His family—to be anointed not with olive oil but the oil of His Spirit!

ROMAN RUINS, THE ANCIENT CITY OF SEBASTE, SAMARIA, PALESTINE
Jesus healed ten lepers in this area of Samaria.

One of them, when he saw he was healed, came back,

praising God in a loud voice . . . . and he was a Samaritan.

LUKE 17:15–16 NIV

Thanks from a Foreigner

The border of Galilee and Samaria was a commonly avoided area where lepers lived together, irrespective of race, united by their common misery. A group of ten of them caught site of Jesus passing through, and though they kept their distance, as was required, they called on Him for mercy. Their request was granted as they obeyed the Mosaic legislation to go and show themselves to the priests who would verify their newfound purity.

But one of them disobeyed momentarily—one of those occasions when law was trumped by spirit. This leper, a Samaritan, turned around and came back to Jesus, falling at His feet, to thank Him for healing him of leprosy. Jesus' further words revealed surprise that only "this foreigner" had returned—suggesting some or all of the other lepers were Jews. Jesus always seemed appreciative when He found faith in places it would not have been anticipated: a Roman centurion, a Canaanite woman, and a Samaritan leper.

Have we become so used to God's blessings that we fail to return to say thank you? Let us take every opportunity to fall at Jesus' feet and thank Him for His mercy, healing, and unwavering love for us.

A Prayer

This is how God showed his love among us:

He sent his one and only Son into the world

that we might live through him.

1 JOHN 4:9, NIV

—◦◦✦◦◦—

Heavenly Father, thank You for allowing me

to experience Your love and presence through

the gift of Your Son, Jesus Christ.